43 A.A.Ballads & Story Poems

Ne bibite et ad consortia ite.*

" It's in the book."

43 A.A. Ballads & Story Poems

Poetic snapshots of unforgettable people you'd like to have known, back in the day.

R.E. Maloney

SPIDER BOOKS PUBLISHING

43 A.A. Ballads
& Story poems

Copyright © 2015 - R.E. Maloney

This book may be ordered through booksellers or by contacting:

Spider Books Publishing, LLC
PO Box 51911
Fort Myers, FL 33994
www.SpiderBooksPublishing.com
(239) 693-DRAW (3729)

ISBN: 978-1-942728-13-9 (Print)
ISBN: 978-1-942728-14-6 (Digital)

Printed in the United States of America

Editing, Cover & Book design: Jennifer FitzGerald - www.MotherSpider.com
Cover image copyrights at dollarphotoclub.com

Table of Contents

Preface

A few months after the expected publication date of this volume of story-poems, ballads (whatever), I will celebrate my 91st birthday. I have been judged by a number of my UA and Medicare care workers to be of sound mind and body, and the statistics say I will be around at least another 17-18 months. Considering the tonnage of tar and nicotine that filtered their way through my lungs, and the barrels of alcohol that were responsible for too many automobile accidents, I would easily put that longevity solidly in the 'miracle' column.

Thank you, Alcoholics Anonymous, for catching up with me in time.

Dedication

I want to dedicate this book to the fifty or so AA members, as well as a very few would-be AA members who are anonymously referred to in this group of poems. In a way, they are stereotypes of the many real people who stuck with me, and taught me the real meaning of fellowship.

Beyond those who shared my addictions, I want especially to say thank you to three wonderful women who, graciously, put up with me, loved me, and did not kick me out: my mother, Delia, and my two wives, Erika and Evelyn. Each put up with me for long periods of time. In between, 1943 to 1948 to be exact, the US Army took over and allowed me extended Asian and European tours.

Also, a thank you is due a US Army Colonel, Medical Corps, who, in 1948, said, "Bob, you're an alcoholic." It was my earliest wake-up call. It's been a long time, but I think the Colonel's name was Chamberlain.

Easy Does It

Introduction

AA Preamble

"Alcoholics Anonymous is a fellowship of men and women who share their experience, strength and hope with each other that they may solve their common problem and help others to recover from alcoholism. The only requirement for AA membership is a desire to stop drinking. There are no dues or fees for AA membership; we are self supporting through our own contributions. AA is not allied with any sect, denomination or politics, organization or institution; does not wish to engage in any controversy, neither endorses nor opposes any causes. Our primary purpose is to stay sober and help other alcoholics achieve sobriety."

The above Preamble to Alcoholics Anonymous, direct from the Big Book, Alcoholics Anonymous, was written by Tom W., then editor of the Grapevine. It first appeared in the Grapevine (The International Journal of Alcoholics Anonymous) in June, 1947.

All of the verses in this volume, whether AA related or not, stem from my actual experiences. Names and places are fictional.

For the record, my first AA meeting in 1958 did not launch me into a 57 year, nonstop, uninterrupted period of sobriety. Nevertheless, my present and continuous sobriety goes back to Valentine's Day, 1977.

Old Jake

I picked him up Tuesdays and Fridays
exactly at seven forty-five.
Each night when he stepped through the door,
I'd read his eyes and they'd say, "Yep, I'm still alive."

Jake had been saying, "I'm ninety-five,"
Since Ponce De Leon found this place,
Here, off the coast of Florida,
And brand new to the human race.

He walked slow and gingerly,
From the door to my old Pontiac.
Efforts to help him were met with snarls
And a wave of his small gunny sack.

Jake had been an electrical engineer;
Many years with RCA,
So he was the natural guy, for sure,
To tend to our mikes and the PA.

None of us were allowed to tinker
With the placement or volume, you see,
Even when the feedback went crazy,
And drove us all up a tree!

This went on for nearly ten years,
Until he started going blind;
He told us he was moving west
To live with a step-niece of some kind.

Then a couple years later, I got a call,
From a hospital ten miles away;
Jake was dying, and his personnel chart
Said to 'notify me, who would want to come and pray.'

It said I was the nearest person,
And would notify his step-niece in Santa Fe
That his estate had been left to the Boy Scouts,
'And I think it's better this way.'

I got to the hospital within the hour,
And was shown to Old Jake's room.
I said, "How are feeling, Jake?"
He said, "Who the fuck are you?"

When I told him who I was,
And that the hospital had called,
He said, "Now I remember, you're the prick
Who sold me the railroad bonds."

I said, "Huh?" He said, "You know the ones;
That hooked up Russia with China;
Or, maybe it was Afghanistan,
Then went through to Asia Minor."

By the time I left, Old Jake was laughing
And I was glad I didn't relate,
That I'd never sold him any bonds
From Russia, China or even Kuwait.

He died that night and I never heard
If the Boy Scouts got his estate;
But I know he died smiling,
And that I had not been too late.

My First Sponsor

I used a bar in Norwood, as a
Home Away From Home,
The juke box played
'When My Blue Moon Turns to Gold Again'
And it was 20 cents for a shot of gin.

That got washed down, with a
Bottle of cold Knick;
The pin ball machine
Paid off in nickels when you won,
And nobody went nuts if you pulled a gun.

One AM, Monday night, 1958, Nick
The Bartender calls, "Time,
Last call is over."
"Have I got time for a telephone call?
Only need a few minutes." Nick, "Maybe five is all."

I get AA Central Service, in Boston,
"Where you calling from?"
I give the gal the number,
"Stay at this phone, you'll get a call back;"
Nick says, "I gotta close up here, Mac."

It's no more than two minutes, when
Damned if it didn't ring,
Nick says, "Hurry up", and
I say, "I'm in a bar in Norwood, Ma'am."
Some guy says, "I'll meet you at this address."

Do I know the Norwood Diner?
I say, sure, you mean now?
He says, "I'm in Norfolk,
It may be half an hour, not even that;
I'm fat and wearing an old Boston Braves hat."

His name was Walter
And, could I owe my life
To a chubby, 60 year old man
Who got out of bed, and spent the night
Listening to a 34 year old full of fright?

Across from the diner was a church
The name? I don't recall;
It might have been Monday
It makes no difference, Walter was always there,
He'd look, and I was always in the same chair.

He took me to meetings
At the Norfolk State Prison;
Those you don't forget,
And talking to the prisoners, some might say,
"Coming to these meetings could reduce my stay."

Walter said, "I know that, Bob,
But, I also know the odds
Are that about half are alkies
And that these seeds we will have sown
Will someday become at least half grown."

I was not a 90-day wonder,
(Like a WW 2 second Lieutenant),
And drank on and off for the next year,
But it turned out that it was not only at the prison
That the seeds of AA had risen.

And for that, I thank you, Walter,
If you're alive you're
At least a hundred twenty-five!
But I'll bet that your sober pigeons, if still alive,
Number at least twice that one twenty-five!

Phillie

The guy was an MIT grad,
A mechanical design engineer.
He said to me, "Bob, my friend,
I sometimes sneak a cold beer."

Now, that was hardly news, folks,
And, 'sneak' was not the right word;
Phillie was about as sneaky
As a raunchy buffalo herd.

He had walked through the door
In March of sixty-three;
Said he worked for I.B.M.,
And that the steps had set him free.

At that time, Phillie was half bald
And getting more so every day,
So, he decides just what he needs,
Is a new chocolate brown toupee.

Now it's December, very same year;
The Friday night meeting's half over,
Phillie comes in (he's often late),
And smelling like lime (maybe clover).

The rug he's wearing is backwards,
Or maybe upside down,
But the guy's not worried about his looks,
(Which compares to a circus clown).

He looks around and catches my eye,
There's an open seat by my side,
So he quietly makes his way over,
Thank God, he's not trying to hide.

The guy is bombed but steady,
I excuse myself, and get to him fast;
I'm afraid his equilibrium
Is in no way going to last.

I steer him out the back door,
And another guy, Carl, comes along;
He's also seen this movie before,
And knows exactly what could go wrong.

"I started with the 3 point 2 stuff,
After getting out of work.
I think I dented another fender,
Guess you think I'm just a jerk."

"Phil, you're what you want to be,
An alcoholic, so you say.
Many of us tell that to ourselves,
Each and every damn day."

Carl G. and I drove him home;
Carl driving his own car,
Me trailing behind as courier,
(It wasn't all that far).

A light was on. His wife was up;
He was hoping she'd be asleep.
We tried to be quiet as possible,
Not make so much as a peep.

We knocked on the door.
His wife, Ellen, was not shocked;
It wasn't the first time this year, that
Phillie had come home fully cocked.

Ellen took charge at this point,
"Thank you, guys, and where was he?"
I said, "He showed at the meeting."
She said, "Some day, he'll run up a tree."

Phillie decided he'd do this himself;
AA was for the weak-kneed;
He once said that it was the devil,
And some day he'd surely get freed.

On New Year's Eve, Phillie met a truck
On the wrong side of Highway I-10,
His car collapsed like an accordion,
And we never saw Phillie again.

<u>Arnold and the Broker</u>

He came to the office in eighty-two
(I was in early that morning)
He said his name was Arnold Fuller
And he seemed to be sort of in mourning.

He said I'd been recommended
By a mutual friend in AA,
And he wanted to work something out, he said,
Before he could "call it a day."

A doctor in Miami had told him,
That he'd better get things together;
His prostate cancer was running wild, and
There was no way it could get any better.

He had moved to Florida in sixty-three,
And had made some wise decisions;
Buying land here, there and everywhere
Now his Will was full of revisions.

He wasn't sure what he had, but knew
It was, in his words, a shit-full.
He'd tried to be his own lawyer,
Because he saw too many as untruthful.

Now, I'm not an attorney, and never was,
But I tried my best to advise him.
And between me and the office guru
(Our manager, else known as "Tight-Ass Tim")

We even called Legal, back in New York,
And they were quick to advise,
That if he trusted just one person
To open a trust fund would be mighty wise.

Mr. Fuller said he'd been sober thirty years,
And his one son, Jake, was also addicted,
But had never believed in AA,
(He said the whole damn crew was afflicted).

At any rate, he had little choice,
But to make the young man his trustee,
And that's exactly what he did;
And a few weeks later he was free.

Soon after Fuller died, Jake shows up at the office.
He's got more wealth than he can handle;
He asked me to help with an account.
(He'd barely lit the last candle!)

I said I would because, "I liked your Dad,
But before you take this dough and go play,
Why don't you think of him for once,
And let me take you to AA."

I was shocked out of my shoes because,
Jake then said, "Thank you, I think I'm ready."
That was twenty years ago, and believe it or not,
Sober Jake Fuller is still an AA "steady!"

Paul

Two marriages and a dozen jobs
Brought Paul P. to our Tuesday meeting,
Slurring his words just a trifle,
While he tried to compose his greeting.

"I guess this is the place," he laughed,
"Where we learn to quit drinking?
The wife's getting ready to dump me;
Yeh, I know that's what she's thinking."

It was a closed discussion meeting;
Middle of August, as I recall,
Four or five guys, couple of gals;
Good thing this group was small.

The new guy looked to be quite well off,
Sharp white shirt and tie;
I knew he was dancing and laughing,
So he wouldn't break down and cry.

Paul then pulled out his wallet,
Before he even took a chair;
"Put your dough away, my friend,
Here, say hello to Ratty O'Hara."

Ratty said, "Throw a buck in the pot, pal,
Later, when it comes around;
But, for now, sit down and listen,
Maybe get a little unwound."

Later, we learned Paul was a singer;
(Not the one with Mary and Peter)
We also learned he loved the ladies, and
Called by his wife, a "lousy cheater."

Three great months past
While Paul stayed clean and dry;
He came to our meetings weekly,
As well as to YANA* near by.

Then one morning I got a call,
"Gotta problem, can we meet?"
"Sure, Paul, how about the diner
Down there on Whistler Street?"

"Elaine called me late last night,"
"That's wife number two, I recall?"
"Yes, she's visiting up in Charlotte and
I could have said no, or maybe stall."

"But, you said fine, I'll be right up,"
"No, I said I'd be up tonight;
I never stopped missing her, Bob,
I think I will be all right."

I then went on to ask him ---
"You want to get laid or stay sober?"
He said he'd prefer to do both;
(And that's after thinking it over.)

I said, "Buddy, it's up to you;
Sometimes it's hard to say no;
But, I'd like to think, if it were me,
I'd find it too risky to go."

Three days later the phone rang,
"You were right, Bob," the man said;
"One thing lead to another and, well
I should have stayed home instead."

Paul died almost 30 years later;
Cancer does not discriminate.
He never took another drink,
And left a beautiful AA mate.

*YANA--You are not alone

<u>BMW Susie</u>

It was probably made before Hitler,
And looked like a metal disaster;
When sober, Susie drove it like Earnhardt
And loaded, she went even faster.

Susie loved her old BMW, and
Maybe even more than Stan.
"But, at least," she said, quietly,
"In bed, I've got the real Stan the Man!"

Susie came around one late summer,
(I think it was seventy-eight)
Her husband wrote trashy novels,
Which easily paid most of the freight.

Small, shapely, maybe a hundred and five,
Permanent grin, always there with a joke;
She said her favorite (besides Stan)
Was a well spiked Rum and Coke.

It took Susie almost fourteen months
To finally gain some sobriety,
But, God blessed this wild little redhead,
('Tho it had come with some improprieties.)

But, LO, in the year 1990 and nine
Susie celebrated twenty years;
This, despite becoming a widow,
Re-marrying and shifting gears!

Susie was also now in Al-Anon;
Her next mate was fairly new,
And he sold new and used autos,
And was known as Toyota Stew.

Susie finally told me her secret, that
She now believed in open lives;
"I can't get my kicks from Stan or booze, Bob,
So I get them with different guys!"

Frank the Barber

Not a single person expected much,
When Frankie came back to the group;
We figured his frau had laid down the law,
"Get sober, or get outta' the loop!"

Frankie's business had tanked long ago;
Who wants a barber that's sloshed?
Maybe lose an ear (sure, get a shave!)
Now he's ready to get tossed.

But Frankie slipped into YANA,
And to an afternoon meeting at that,
and, Heads turned inadvertently,
Old Sparky even took off his hat!

Some gal said, "Frank's got the record
Of coming back after a slip."
Her husband, Joe, said, "Delia,
They were more like abandoning ship."

Frank grabbed a seat at the back, and
I figured he'd be gone before the prayer,
But each time I take a quick glance,
Son of a gun, the old drunk is still there.

Now, Frankie is closer to fifty
Than he is to forty-five,
And around that age it gets tougher
To stay out of your favorite dive.

He was over six foot two
And fat covered both belly and ass;
Once a star at a well know school,
Known to throw one hell of a pass!

After the meeting, he came over to shake,
Then quickly he said, "Can we talk?"
I said, "Follow me back to my place,
We'll get a sandwich, maybe take a little walk."

We strolled through a small garden,
Across the street from my house,
There he told his story, while
I stayed still as a mouse.

"I haven't got much time, Bob,
And I don't mean just tonight;
Smoking, booze, what not and,
Well, there's not much left that's right."

He went on to say the doctors
Had given him, maybe, a few weeks;
The Big C had hit him here and there,
And they were even spreading leaks.

"I want to die with some sobriety
Even if it's days, not years;
I know there's nothing you can do,
And I sure don't want buckets of tears."

Less than a month went by, and
Frank went to three meetings a week;
Open meetings, his wife came along,
Then somebody asked him to speak.

It was a Sunday night Open Meeting,
The chair said the words, "Here's Frank D."
His wife, Emmy said, "Frankie, wake up,"
I said, "Emm, I think our Frankie's now free."

Somewhere in China
Jan.-1945

<u>My Darling, Annie</u>

Honey, I miss you so, should I go
AWOL, so they'll send me home?
Yes, I know that's wrong, but it's been so long,
And I can't stand this being alone.

I want to hear, your voice with a tear;
Saying that you miss me, too;
This place is dreary, and I'm too weary
To do what I have to do.

Tonight my group, of all the troops;
Is heading for (something)-ing;
The Japs have the road, but our big load
Has got to get through to Kunming.

I've got to run, (it won't be much fun,)
But maybe the war will end soon,
And we can make love, under the stars above,
While watching a full Christmas moon.

I love you,
                    Your Billy

Jan. 27, 1945

<u>Dear Billy--</u>

I don't want to write, this letter tonight,
But, write it I must, and right away;
No, it wouldn't be right, to spend this night
With my new husband, Tommy LeGray.

Tommy got out, and I have no doubt
He'll love and be good to me;
I know it sounds corny, but I am so horny
It's driving me up a tree!

Good luck on your trip!
Annie

Rolls Royce Jack

He'd been at the Toronto Convention,
Back there in 'sixty-five,
The best of them all, he told me,
And this, he said, was why:

"That's when the Responsible Pledge
Was introduced," he said
"Ten Thousand ex-drunks said it aloud,
While my eyes got teary and red."

(Basically, the Pledge says,
"Whenever anyone, anywhere,
Reaches out for help,
It's our job to be there.")

Rolls Royce Jack drove a Renault,
One built before that convention;
But, he always talked about "my Rolls"
And his British Railroad Pension.

Now, no one doubted "Boston Jack",
(As he was also known some places),
And his sobriety date was never in doubt
(Like it was in many cases!)

He'd "seen the light" in Salem, Mass.
Not long after World War Two;
Many old souls from that area
Said, "He loved his U.K. Dark brew."

The group once threw him a party,
To mark his fiftieth year
Of continuous sobriety;
(He had joked, "How about just one beer?"

You see, about ninety-five percent
Of people who belong to our group,
Are also friendly "off the field"
And part of the program loop.

Not so, our stoic Rolls Royce Jack,
Who always came alone,
Never spoke of any other family,
Other than the one we called "our own."

Jack died last year at 96,
And we realized we never knew
Much of anything about him;
Except his love for the Rolls and Brew.

One old broad, however; one
Who came around now and then,
Gave us an address she said was his,
And not shared by any of the men.

It took the better part of an hour
To find this old ten acre farm;
Shoddy buildings all over the place,
A sign out front, "Manor De Calm."

It was there we found the Rolls;
In fact, we found fourteen!
(One or two looked like they might run)
But, it was still a very weird scene.

Jack had left a will, all right,
But it eventually wound up in court;
The estate belonged to a gal in Wales
Who wrote, "We once shared a bottle of port."

Six months after his passing,
A friend and I took a ride,
Out to the old farm house
And the Rolls where the old man died.

Yep, they had found him in the front seat,
The big book was at his side;
I suppose he had been planning
On taking his last buggy ride.

A year or so later the place was sold,
By the lady from Wales, to the town;
For something like ten thousand dollars---
"Miss Wales" couldn't turn it down!

There's a morale here somewhere,
But I don't know where to look;
The old guy died happy
Although nothing like, "by the book."

Smoke Filled Rooms

Didn't matter, be it library, church or school;
Maybe a private company, or
An old Coca-Cola plant dining room,
Maybe a shack by the Home for the Poor.

If this place didn't allow smoking
They were not on the list
As a possible AA meeting place;
(The members would all get pissed!)

This was not only the norm
It was more like an unwritten law;
If there was an exception anyway,
It was some country I never saw.

Now, I never attended meetings,
In Salt Lake City, or Ogden;
And I'd be surprised if AA was as big
In those two cities as, say, Boston.

It was not 'till the eighties, when
There was even isolated talk;
I was once at a quarterly members' meeting
When one person brought it up as a lark.

Smoking was considered an absolute must,
By a few, even in two thousand three,
One group even held a secret meeting
So there would not be a vote for "smoke-free."

Well, what do you know, it's all turned around,
And if there's smoking, here or there
I guess that it's in a wheat field,
Or, the middle of China, somewhere.

So, "Changes" is more than just a bad song;
It's sometimes right and sometimes wrong
Like if this f-----g computer was suddenly trash,
I could go back to my Royal, and save mucho cash!

So, my bottom line, (if you give a shit), says
If you'd kept going to AA meetings,
where there was still smoking,
And even if you'd quit yourself,
you'd have been cremated long ago,
and Buster, I'm Not Joking!

Rosanne

They said she'd had the sweetest
Of pop singers golden voices;
She said, "I liked the bright lights,
And I'll make my own dumb choices."

She'd married twice, then once too often,
The third to an absolute bum;
By this time, she was an old twenty-three
With the worst days yet to come.

How could booze be a problem?
This gal was only a kid;
They said she'd prowled the local bars,
And accepted the highest bid.

So, she got a ride to Florida;
Try something else, she thought.
Got a job in Casey's Beach Saloon.
('Twas a lonely battle she fought.)

Until one night, on a Naples Beach,
She started crying and couldn't stop;
And the sobs and wails were soon picked up
By a beach cruising Naples cop.

The cop showed her to the hideout,
Where she lived with some hop head jerk,
And made her promise to stay there
'Till about six, when he got off work.

Norm had been in the program, but
Only a few months, more or less,
But, he knew who to summon;
This was made for Tinker Bell Tess.

Nearly a year after Rosanne was found,
A wreck on a Florida beach,
She was in a Nashville studio, and
Her voice no longer a screech.

Exactly one year from her magic day,
She flew back to the Florida coast, and
There she celebrated her first sober year,
With Tess and a Root Beer float.

The Old Garage Gang

The craziest thing about this old place,
(And that's saying more than you want to know)
Is that it was there on a main highway;
Gulf Coast Florida, with wicked traffic flow!

Two old buildings, set back 100 feet,
Surrounded by mid to high class mobile homes.
Stores like seven-eleven and Chinese Chow,
No parks, apartments, or lofty steeple domes.

Sal's was a radiator repair shop, and
Radiator Sal was owner and main mechanic;
There was always a group hanging about and
Always an air of feverish panic.

"It'll be done when I call you, lady!
I've only one helper and two hands,
My other guy's over at the clinic,
Something about swollen lymph glands."

"Thanks, Hon, I'll deliver it tomorrow,
No, I can't stay for a drink or two;
You know that stuff is poison to me,
But, I'd go for a cup of your stew."

Hanging around reading a "True Lust" mag,
Sammy Horseshoe was in the back,
Needing a wee-wee, so he did just that; but,
Lacking in proper facilities, was this fifty year old shack.

Well, who walks in, at this particular point,
But this Jamaican cop with a smile on his kisser,
He says, "We got a phone call from Mrs. Carey;
"She's complaining about a drunken pisser."

"Sammy," Sal hollers, "Roberto the Cop is here,
He's got a ticket for you, I trust.
And, the next time, for Jesus, and my sake,
Piss in the sink like the rest of us!"

Lawyer Thorn Meets Boston Blackie

Everyday, even weekends, he sat on his ass,
Hoping someone might come through his door;
Or, even, more likely, the phone to ring
Maybe someone rich, or even someone poor.

His office was on Sanibel Island;
He went there soon after he passed the bar.
Everybody was rich, famous and really old.
He arrived in a new rental car.

His wife, Peachy, got in the swing of it;
Parties, classy clothes, lots of attention;
While he sat reading law books,
You'd think law was a new invention!

He joined the clubs and was mostly ignored
They asked him who his Dad might be;
He gave them a line of bullshit
And an old Boston family tree.

A neighbor once asked him to play some golf;
(The course had more water than land)
He'd had two lessons in Orlando, so
The stakes only cost him a grand.

Then one day, right out of the blue
Boston Blackie Two comes walzing in.
He says, "Mr. Thorn, I'm Blackie,
And I'm not sure just where to begin."

Lawyer Thorn said, "How about the beginning?"
And hoped that didn't sound fresh.
Blackie sat down, opened his jacket;
A man who would always impress.

"I represent a consortium, of unusual investors,
Who are privy to important information.
Like, names and habitations of smugglers
Who do illegal immigrations."

"Well, Mr. Blackie, why don't----"
"Because there's no money in telling the cops
They round them up, they're off to jail
And we, maybe, get 50 bucks a pop."

Well, the idea came rolling out
And, to Thorn, it sounded dandy
He'd rat them out, one at a time,
And be the only mouthpiece handy!

Mrs. Thorn doesn't worry about money anymore;
Not since Boston Blackie moved in.
He's selling condos on West Gulf Drive
Thorn took his graft, and not seen since.

But the Florida bar guys are still looking,
As are the smugglers, out on bond,
They're wondering where their 2 million retainer fee,
And that fucking lawyer, have suddenly up and gone!

Hammy

He'd say, "I'm Joe M." but we called him Hammy;
We'd heard that his name was either Wald or Hall,
We never knew, nor did anyone care,
It was a little confusing, but that's about all.

What was a big mystery was his walking stick;
We knew that Hammy had been shot twice;
In one of his talks he said it happened in France, but
Later, he said, "while shooting dice."

Angie the Angel said neither was the case,
That Hammy had been hunting down Maine;
Some guy from Bangor yelled, "Poachers!"
In seconds, Hammy was feeling the pain.

A kangaroo court cleared the farmer,
Then decided to fine Hammy and his friends;
The hunting season or no hunting season,
He thought, "Some day I'll get my revenge."

This was in the fall of sixty-eight;
There was all kinds of trouble in 'Nam,
And while students were raising holy hell,
Hammy was thinking of an old Maine farm.

In the winter of nineteen seventy-three,
Hammy went shopping one cold afternoon.
He told Delia, his wife, 'don't wait up'
Then added, "But I should be back pretty soon."

Hammy came back the next morning,
And packed his Mauser away;
He said to Delia, "That's that,"
and, "I'll tell you the rest some day."

A couple years later, Hammy was gone,
And his wife came to our meeting in tears;
She said, "you were his very best friends,
And gave him his very best years."

"He would want you to know what happened;
The truth about his leg, you see.
He was shot by a guy from Bangor;
So that's where he went back in seventy-three

Hammy knew he'd been shot on purpose,
And had vowed to "kill that prick."
So off he went in his pick up truck,
His gun strapped to his walking stick.

But when he confronted the farmer, he said,
"I came here to cut off your nuts.
When I left my home in Arlington,
I hated your fuckin' guts."

"But when I got out of my truck,
Out there by that old apple tree,
I thought of what has kept me sober,
And I think we can both go free!"

With that, Hammy stuck out his hand,
And the old farmer broke down crying;
He said, "I been praying for this Joe,
And if I said different, I'd only be lying."

It turned out that the farmer
Had been drinking "a wee too much."
It was becoming a big ugly problem
With the wife, the kids and such.

He had taken Hammy to the kitchen;
Where the stove gave the only heating.
"You know you've got a problem, Ted?
Tonight we're going to a meeting."

Delia said, "I'm going to go see old Ted,
And see how he's doing these days.
Do you guys think that would be OK?
Maybe sort of mend our ways."

Angie the Waitress happened by,
And heard the whole conversation.
She sidled by, whispered to Delia,
"It could be a real fun occasion!"

The Old Howard Theater
Howard Street, Boston, Mass.

The Old Howard had a smell, right from hell;
But we high school kids could care less;
As long as the strippers showed their nippers
They were passing the acid test.

The fleet's been sunk, we're all getting drunk,
Even 'tho we're only sixteen;
We're skipping school, and think that's "cool"
(Although "cool" had not yet made the scene.)

We'd usually meet, just down the street
From Somerville High School, you see;
There we'd count, the total amount
Because you didn't see Ann Corio for free!

The system was sloppy, and one could copy
Any old excuse on a new sheet;
Teachers were going, most not knowing,
When, again, we would all meet.

Haven't been in Scollay Square, (is it still there?)
But I can still see the old cart-path alley,
Trash on the street, characters you'd meet;
Guys named O'Brien, Kelley and O'Malley.

Three shows a day, and you could stay
As long as you damn well pleased.
A movie, the show, then another,
How long can a teen-ager be teased?

The cost? For that I'm a little lost,
But forty cents comes to mind;
Add a dime for the carfare sometimes,
And it was as good a day as you might find!

Now, for some reason, whatever the season,
It was always a Monday we'd pick;
Maybe the price, (maybe less lice),
Or, maybe just easier to be sick.

Well, we finally got nailed, not because we failed,
But because a teacher finally caught on;
His named was Grimes, and he spoiled our good times,
And followed us one Monday morn.

Yep, there he was, just like the fuzz;
Writing our names on his pad.
He right away mentioned, serious detention,
But, he didn't seem really that mad.

He said, "Get B's and A's, the rest of the way
And we'll forget the entire affair.
The you can graduate, clean and sedate
And ready to be shipped "Over There!"

The Old Timer

What was his name? That's a shame,
I can't remember, so I'll say, Ray;
Half of a wife and hubby team,
Thanks to their courage and AA.

Ray had quit, (bit by bit)
Going to meetings, I was told,
But this was an anniversary affair,
And man, was this guy old!

Corky said, "He's the speaker, and
I've only seen him once before;
He's about ninety, and a little flighty
But he's old AA, right to the core."

His wife was Betty, and still a steady,
In both AA and Al Anon;
She had over 60 years sobriety
Hell, most of us had yet to be born!

A writer Walt, brought the noise to a halt,
And said, "OK let's get started."
At which point, from the back of the hall,
Ray lifted one old leg and farted!

From each end of the floor, there came a roar
And I looked around and there's Betty,
Whacking the old man with a Pepsi can,
While Walt's yelling, "Steady folks, steady!"

This was a big crowd, and they were still loud
When Walt says, "We've got a great speaker!"
And the serenity prayer, made some repair
(Although recited a little bit weaker.)

The Preamble and Steps, (almost like reps)
Were duly observed by a member,
Who did a good job, considering the mob
Would be laughing come next December!

Ray's introduction was like a seduction,
Inviting Ray to take over the show;
And, take over he did, like some little kid;
A kid who would never grow.

Betty was appalled, and often called
To Ray, right from the floor:
"That's right, it was the night,
You called me a goddamn whore!"

Ray would continue with a weird retinue
Of stories only an old drunk could tell,
While Betty got madder than the proverbial hatter,
As the stories got crazy as hell!

This went on for much too long,
Although I'll admit it was good shit;
Him crowing away, she up and down in her chair,
The rest of us ready for the next bit.

Finally it ended, and we all pretended
That we understood what he'd been saying;
While Betty calmed down (and came around),
Alternately laughing and praying.

Both are long gone, and it would be wrong
To wish they were still around;
What would they be? No, I'm glad to believe,
I'll see them some day under ground.

Yes, they were just a pair, but always there,
To help another lush get free.
Eccentric, not really, just old and dearly
Beloved by other AA's; don't you agree?

The Ballad of Patty P.

She came, she saw, not a single flaw
in her zany plan to move on;
Boston was cold, she's getting old,
"Let's see what I got I can pawn."

Patty had been sober, she said, for over
thirty-five years in A.A.
"I'll look around, but I think I've found
The place where I might want to stay."

It was off the coast, unknown to most
of the Florida touristy gang;
Her Packard could stay, safe all day,
While she sun-bathed, golfed and sang.

And Patty had starred, by working hard,
as a Radio City Rockette;
Yes, she'd been to the post, more often than most, but
She was still an intriguing coquette.

Now, equally needed, and not ever impeded,
was her need for her A.A. Friends;
She'd done her twelve steps (with many reps)
and enjoyed her 'making amends.'

Then she met Hoaky, nicknamed Smokey,
(he hacked about two packs a day);
Well, Smokey struck out, and began to pout
"Bob, I'm in love, what else can I say."

"You can say 'I quit', and quickly admit
Those butts are costing you too much;
You can trade cancer, for this little dancer;
So get rid of that fucking crutch!"

Well, Hoaky quit smoking, and I'm not joking,
When I say it came to pass,
That lives were saved and a marriage made;
Between an old ex-drunk and a cute little Rockette lass.

I Coulda' Been A Hooker!

I put up with three past hubbies;
All moved in; came and went;
One like a rail, two were tubbies
All three had this boozy scent.

Met two in a bar, one at church;
Two I tossed, one found another,
And there I was, left in the lurch,
Then I said, "Daisy, why bother?"

The craziest thing, I'm thinking,
I'm known as a pretty good looker;
And if it wasn't for all this drinking
I'd made a pretty good hooker!

'Course, it might be a trifle late
And even if I'm finally free
To go on line for some kind of date;
After all I am eighty-three!

Edie and Ray

Raymond C. was a happy, happy, drunk,
And Edie was a happy, happy, mate;
They had many a happy, happy, time together,
And of that, there was no debate.

This was back in the cold war days,
When Ray was a rocket scientist;
A PHD from a top rate school,
One among the very highest.

He drank because he liked it, he said,
And rejected the "alcoholic" label;
Even when he often drank himself
Under the nearest bar or table.

Then they married and a little one came,
And Edie switched her men;
Raymond Two took center stage,
And she said, "let's do that again!"

You bet, Ray was heard to respond,
And sure enough she had another;
And the younger Ray was giddy,
At the idea of having a brother.

Meanwhile, Big Ray grew further away;
In his home there was no place,
While Edie was not often available;
And love? Not even a trace!

Pretty soon, two lovers were four,
Both Edie and Ray had another;
Each knew, each could care less.
(They were both living deep under cover.)

Enter Ray's boss back in Phoenix,
The guy who ran the whole show;
The man responsible for the rockets,
And the one who needed to know.

He summoned Ray to the Home Office
Where he told him, that was it;
He'd watched the guy long enough, now,
And had taken quite enough of his shit.

Ray was now out on his ass, with
His wife shacked up with some freak;
His own kids hardly knew him,
Talk about being up the creek!

He got back home and made a call;
A friend of a friend of a friend.
The new guy asked him a question,
"Just what do you intend?"

"To get my life on track," Ray said,
"My wife, my kids, my honor."
"I'll pick you up at seven tonight;
I'm right around the corner"

Not long ago, Ray had an anniversary;
He celebrated forty-five years
Of continuous sobriety;
His wife and kids were in tears.

They had a little get together;
One of his grand sons wanted to know,
"What do you do at these meetings, Gramps;
Is it like a TV show?"

"No. Michael, there's a story, or
We just say hi to each other in greeting,
Then we remind each other, sometimes,
'Don't drink, and go to meetings'."

My Dad

"I'm Dick, and I'm an alcoholic."
Those words he never said,
Unless it was early in life,
And long before he was wed.

But, from the day his mother asked
That he go and take the Pledge,
There was only one medicinal jug,
Sitting high on a pantry ledge.

I should know, Dick was my Dad
And the only alky I ever knew,
Who stayed sober from age nineteen,
Not even touching the old home brew.

To me, his story came in bits,
Never from his own words;
He never spoke of booze to me
Like he did about the bees and the birds.

My older sister said it had to do
With getting tossed out of a seminary;
It seemed he was a real hell-raiser;
Never known as "sedentary"

He also had played pro baseball,
In the old New England League;
Getting paid, under a new name,
He called it, "a bit of intrigue."

Since I was not quite eighteen
When the war broke out in forty-one,
My own affliction was barely noted,
'though he knew I liked to have fun!

So for the next, almost six years,
We talked mostly by mail,
And my antics to him were unknown
And then he got sick and even quite frail.

Then came nineteen forty-eight
When I wrote from Germany that June;
I was going to be married in August
And be home after our honeymoon.

I told the folks she was German,
And enclosed a picture she had.
I said she also had a cute little boy
And I'd try and be a good dad.

In the summer of 'forty-four,
My brother's plane had gone down
Out there in the South Pacific
He later died, and the pilot was never found.

Germans and Japanese citizens,
Were not on our favorites list;
So when I wrote that letter, I wondered
If Mom and Dad will get pissed.

A couple weeks later, I got my answer
The letter was addressed to Erika,
My beautiful bride-to-be,
Written by my own dying father:

"We feel like we know you,
because we know our son, and
We trust him when he says,
Dad, she's the one. So please know
He'll make you happy, and we'll
Love you like our own."

That was my Dad.

Blind BB

"I'm Blind BB, and I'm an alcoholic"
The opening was like the rest of us,
(I'm so and so, then the alcoholic bit;)
From there he spoke like a true lush.

"Let's get the blindness out of the way.
I put a gun to my head one night,
Pulled the trigger, and here I stand,
With maybe ten percent of my sight."

BB went on to tell of the D Ts,
That brought that night about;
He'd been drinking his Sneaky Pete,
Topped off with a case of Stout.

Then a good ten years later,
And BB's back under the bridge;
That's literally where they found him,
Stuffed in a big Westinghouse fridge.

He was staying warm, he said;
Someone else said it was 80 degrees,
but BB said, "so what, you jerk,
Do you want your old pal to freeze?"

There are not many that refuse
To "get with the program," once exposed;
But BB was one of the unlucky ones
And this sad-shit story's now closed.

The Slip

"Nobody said, it's a silk-covered bed,
Or you're 'gonna get something for nothing,
You've got a choice, a push cart or Rolls Royce;
Man, you're really something!"

We were in Fat Eddie's diner;
I could barely see Tim through the smoke
Nearly two AM, and I'm sure his wife Jem
Is getting sick of this old joke.

"You lose your job, then decide to rob
A fucking grocery store;
They pick you up, you're in your cups
Now, you say there's even more?"

They tossed Tim in jail (he's now out on bail)
I'm sure it's his first hard jolt
With the forces of law and order,
And I'm afraid he might simply bolt.

"It was only a slip." "Man, you're really a pip."
How many times have I heard that?
"It was only a skunk, again getting drunk,"
I'm thinking: "This could be your last time at bat!"

"I've tried to fast, even gone to mass,
And talked to you and my Priest;
But, 'First Things First', won't quell the thirst,
It's either a famine or feast."

"I'll talk to your wife, but it's your life,
Not mine, not hers, not your kids;
But even God's had enough of your bullshit stuff
And I'm no auctioneer taking bids."

I went on to say, "there is no way
For you to stay sober alone.
I want you to go, to a meeting, you know,
Every night and also to phone."

"You can call me or Jack T.
And tell us which meeting
And I'll want you to speak, in maybe a week,
Even if it's only a brief greeting."

For thirty straight nights, someone caught sight
Of Timmy at some meeting or other;
Then, thirty more. (he was keeping score)
Then one night he brought his mother!

It's now forty years, and an ocean of tears,
That Tim sat in that cell;
And three generations, (not all were sensations)
But at least one, who finally got well!

Steve

There he sat, unable to drive,
Sipping a beer, and still alive.
His leg in a cast,
Pondering his past,
It was even money he'd not survive.

One thousand miles, he had come
"Finally made it; hi ya, Mom!
Got a ride from Daytona,
Not much fun, bein' a loner,
Not much fun, bein' a bum."

The trucker who brought him,
A guy Steve called Slim,
Said, "I saw the two canes
So I slid over two lanes,
and I guess it was done on a whim!"

Well, Steve did stick around,
But then headed west-ward bound;
Hobbling, but with only one cane,
There he was, on the road again
Headed for another, more lively town.

Six months later, a ringing phone
and I thought it had another tone;
And it did, because, right out of the blue,
(And somehow Evie had a clue)
Steve was saying, "I'm no longer alone."

He said her name was Diane,
And they were working on a plan
To get clean and sober together;
(They were surely birds of a feather)
Evie said, "With God and AA, you can!"

Old Ron

On an island retreat, with no County Seat,
Or Government of any sort,
Old Ron retired, and was soon admired
For his supply of hard-to-get Port.

(He had quite a Biz, "old" wine, but sans fizz)
While the locals smiled and looked on,
Boats would come in, all ready to begin
Loading their wine, then were soon gone.

In those old days, one found the Cay,
And maneuvered around a huge rock;
You anchored in close, by a new white post,
Where you paid Old Ron for your stock.

You got one taste, then paid by the case,
(Never one jug at a time)
Everyone knew, this was home brew,
And each sale was likely a crime.

But this old fart was much too smart,
And knew the sheriff and his gal;
There was no way that some fine day,
He'd be screwed by his buddy, Big Sal.

So Ron was on top, and at 40 a pop,
It was getting to be quite a bounty;
Until a new election, made his island a section,
Of the new, restricted, Gulf county.

Lo, the tax people came, and ended the game
That Old Ron had so well played,
Buying grape juice, for maybe a deuce,
And never drinking the rot gut he made!

I guess no one died, and many people lied,
And no one worried much about it;
And that's how Old Ron, survived the Big Con,
And said, "Well, no one ever got drunk from it!"

Grandmothers

My grandmothers were old when I came along;
By the time I was five they had died;
I never knew them to sing me a song,
Or take me out for a ride.

My parents were always busy,
What with a bunch of kids to raise,
But I got lots of loving, for sure,
And even a lot of nice praise.

But nobody could talk about slavery,
Or what all those wars were about;
Why Mr. Galento was a guinea,
And Mrs. Schultz was a kraut.

I once asked an aunt, who lived in the south,
Why blacks and whites lived apart;
She said she wasn't really sure, but
"Maybe they're not as smart."

Well, I know Aunt Betty was flakie,
But that made no sense at all;
I thought that my mother's mother
Would call it "a mite off the wall".

My grandmother Keyes was a Hammond
Grandma Maloney from the Bear Tribe;
Grandfather Keyes founded a bank,
And Granddad Maloney was hard to describe.

Somehow I wonder how I might have grown,
Sitting around on the floor,
Listening to the four of them gabbing, and
Telling stories from long before.

So, kids, count your blessings
If you've got one or two
Of those from past generations;
To help with whatever you do.

No one pays any attention to Fathers' Day, so I suggest we
change it to Grannies' Day

An Al-Anon Angel

Always a part, and sometimes the heart,
Of a couple of Al-Anon groups,
This sweet, renowned, with eyes so brown,
Could make any man jump through hoops!

For a very long while, there was always the smile
That greeted every drunk or their mate;
There was always a quick hug, even for the lug,
Who might not have smelled that great!

In the winter of eighty-two, with not much to do,
Evie was checking out a new strip mall;
She noticed this guy, who quietly said "Hi."
She'd seen him at a meeting last fall!

Now, Christmas was a day, or maybe two, away;
This new AA guy was alone, she knew,
So she decided, then quickly invited,
This new fellow Corky, for her Christmas beef stew!

Now, just to complete, and fill another seat,
She called her old fried Lucy;
So, the four enjoyed, and Corky was buoyed,
With a dinner both hearty and juicy!

Alas, came the day, when Evie could not stay
Any longer at home with me;
Sharp pains in her head, dementia, they said;
Ten years later, my dear Evie was freed.

Max

Max was a very old man when I knew him,
And that was back in sixty-four;
Long retired, ridden with arthritis,
An AA man to the core.

When he finally collapsed at 90,
He was still sponsoring one or two men;
He even worked with a gal or two,
(And each time, said "never again!")

When I moved away from the area,
I had known him nearly five years;
And in that length of time, I'm sure,
He'd way-laid hundreds of fears.

They came to him shaking,
Some from fear, but also some with D Ts;
He put them to bed, let them sweat,
Made them some broth, maybe green tea.

Then the phone calls, early the next day;
To wives or mothers, "Yes, he's OK."
Or, "You better leave him here with me;
It may be better that way."

A bath, some soup, a lot of caffeine,
And then to a meeting that very night;
Where he'd shake a dozen or two hands
And then hear, "Buddy, it'll be all right!"

Arnold Crump

Feb. 14, 1944
APO 545 - Bath, Me.

Arnie, why aren't you writing?
We've not heard from you in weeks
Are you out somewhere fighting?
Those fucking German creeps?

Here, it's cold, and plenty of snow,
Daddy's out fishing right now;
They cut a big hole in our little lake
To get there you need a damn plow.

I want to say Happy Valentine's Day;
Do they have that shit over there?
I hear the French are big on that stuff.
But, maybe these days they don't care.

Anyway, Peter didn't give me a card,
And I'm thinking of getting a new beau;
What would you think about Frederick?
Of course, he's just twelve, you know.

Well, I hope there's more excitement there
Than we've got here at home;
And make sure you send Ma a postcard,
Especially when you get to Rome.

Love from your little sister,
     ---Nan

(oops, Dad just came in and wants me to tell you to be careful.
He says, "stay away from wild women, especially in Rome.)

Arnie,
 I never told you about rubbers, but I guess the army has
taken care of that. Right?
 Happy hunting,
 Pops

Antique Andy

Andy came up from across the border,
"A little old coal mining town," he said;
Looking for work that wasn't there,
"My home town is really dead."

Andy got a job at a Ford plant,
And for a month or two things went well;
He'd sent his wife some needed cash,
And was thinking straight, you could tell.

We later found out he had gone to AA,
Back in old Kentucky;
He'd then been sober about two weeks,
And was starting to feel pretty lucky.

On his fourth or fifth new payday,
Andy thought he'd go out to eat;
He'd made a couple of friends now,
And maybe he could finally treat.

When the three guys ordered,
Andy heard himself say, "Me too."
He'd have just one beer, you see, and
What harm could one beer do?

When Andy ordered the third,
He said, to himself, "I'll leave half."
And he did just that, and was proud;
Even had a little laugh.

For the next month or so, they said,
Andy had one "now and then,"
He was living cheap, sending money home,
Then he took the boys out again.

They brought him to Max screaming
(They'd been called by the cops around noon.)
He'd been gone three days and nights.
Max said, "He stops, or he's dead pretty soon."

Max called the hospital right away
And Andy was soon in detox;
Where he stayed about 36 hours,
Or until Max showed up with some socks!

He also brought some underwear, and
Andy said, "I gotta go to work."
Whereupon, Max said, "Fella,
Stop talking like some asshole jerk."

That night Andy went into D Ts,
Max had just started to doze,
When he heard the guy screaming,
"There's snakes coming out of my toes!"

Somehow they made it through the night;
(They say Max had to give him a shot)
The old guy had his ways and means,
Things he'd learned, experienced, or bought.

Max made a call to the Ford plant,
And made Andy tell the story;
"Always best to be honest," he told Andy
"No matter how dirty and gory."

They did two-a-day meetings
For about the next two weeks;
Max was bored out of his mind,
But had stopped his mid-night "peeks."

Twenty years later, Max is gone;
Andy has been sober ever since;
He buys, restores and sells antique cars--
(Ask him about snakes; watch him winch!)

He also will sponsor most anyone new,
And speaks each year on that date,
When he'd watched the snakes come closer,
"How can anyone ever feel this great!"

Andy's farm almost borders a Great Lake,
It's kept neat even with the old cars;
On the side of one barn there's a wooden sign,
"Don't drink, go to meetings, and
STAY OUT OF THOSE
FUCKING BARS!"

Call Me Will

Call me Will, he said, that first night;
"Will Go", he said, giggling (alone)
"But, only here," he continued,
"I don't have a telephone."

"Looking to buy a Rainbow,?" he asked,
"That's the vacuum rage, you know;
Call this number, ask for Will,
Tell who answers where, and when, you want me to show."

He said he offered five bucks,
To anyone giving him a referral;
Then another ten, he went on,
If, and when, the sale was final.

It may be a lady, answering the phone,
His girl friend, name of Toni;
It was not only her phone, he said,
But so was the three year old pony!

The horse lived in the house,
Right along with Toni and Will;
Brave Boy had his own bedroom,
With his own window sill.

His room abutted the kitchen,
And placed right above the sink,
Was a sliding door so you wouldn't miss
Brave Boy's morning stink.

His main door opened to a hallway
That led to a messy back yard;
His clomp, clomp, clomp was like gun shots
That keeps everyone always on guard.

Will rode this nag every morning,
Good weather and bad, through the clover,
Then around the neighborhood,
All the while staying happy and sober.

So, you newcomers, it's all up to you,
And you don't have to be "in the loop,"
To have a life that's yours to enjoy;
just "Don't drink, go to meetings,"
(And stay clear of Brave Boy's poop!)

Cornwall Bill

He was canned in mid-April,
Came to the program that same May;
By November he had six months
Of sobriety in AA.

That was in nineteen sixty,
A lot has happened since then;
Like meeting his new sponsor
Truly a man among men.

Bill's transfer came in early sixty-one;
He arrived in his new town alone,
His wife and son back east;
He'd said, "Honey, don't worry, I'll phone."

On Friday, Bill went to a meeting
At one of the churches near by;
He met the guys and ladies, then said,
"See you next week," to some guy.

That guy turned out to be Grady,
An electrical contractor, he said;
The next morning, Bill's phone rang,
At the Motel, he was barely out of bed.

"Hope you don't mind my calling,
You mentioned the Holiday Inn,
Well, we're going to an Elyria meeting;
Can we pick you up about ten?"

Now, if you've been around,
And have some years behind you,
You'll know what these guys are up to,
But, at the time, Bill had no clue.

This guy's 500 miles from home, with
Only a few short months of sobriety;
His first weekend away, "who knows,"
He might look for a little variety.

Bill went with them on Saturday,
And they picked him up Sunday night, too;
Do you know of any other group,
That would know just what to do?

Twenty years later, Bill's moved again;
The phone rings and it's Grady's wife;
"Bill, I'm sorry to tell you,
He's gone, Bill, but what a wonderful life."

"He died in his sleep, Bill, and
At least a hundred guys came by;
Some are with me right now, and
A few of them want to say, 'hi'."

For five years Grady was his sponsor,
Always at the end of his phone,
He talked with the guys for almost an hour;
When he hung up, he was suddenly alone.

But, then his dear wife, Evie,
Slipped into the room by his side;
(He knew she'd guessed all along)
And had had herself a good cry.

Now, Evie had only once met Grady,
And that was not in the old early days;
But the AA family is special,
No matter who "goes" and who "stays."

That evening, about nine-thirty,
Evie picked up the phone;
She called Grady's wife, Betty, and said,
"I don't want you to be all alone."

An Old and Tired C-43

When the left engine stopped
I could hear my heart pound,
The co-pilot said, "We got lucky;
There's rice paddies all around."

The edge of the Himalayan mountains
Is not where you'd normally choose
To have one of your two engines stop
(Up to now it had been a nice cruise.)

You leave India for Kunming,
And go right over the top
Five hundred miles, or so,
Peaks, rice paddies, not many places to stop.

The Air Force Captain cut in to say,
"We picked a pretty good place
We're within a mile of the Burma Road,
And, that's our one saving Grace!"

"How far are we from Kunming," I asked.
He said, "Probably fifty miles,
But you'll have to camp or bivouac
Until, the next convoy comes along single file."

He put us down smartly and smoothly,
When we debarked, we almost sunk;
The paddy field water was to our knees
And I can't describe how it stunk.

I told him I had been on Convoy Three,
And maybe I'd know someone;
He said, "Kid, I like your attitude,
But, I don't think it'll be much fun."

Our plane carried only a few supplies
A few cases of beer and wine,
It was mostly filled with soldiers, and I asked,
"Can we take a few jugs of wine?"

He said, "Help yourselves, it won't last long
These hills are full of rebel tribes,
And they already know where we are
I think they're born with those vibes."

The co-pilot then said, "I'll stay with the plane."
The pilot responds, "The hell you will."
His buddy says, "Maybe the radio will work."
The Captain replied,
"Will that be before or after you get killed?"

Everyone grabbed two bottles of wine,
And strapped them to their packs;
We sloshed along in a foot of water
Some men pulling gunny sacks.

We reached the road just before dark
One Sergeant says, "That's that, we're stuck;
No trucks are going to be coming along now,
And until then we're just shit out of luck."

Soon, one of the guys spots a small trail,
And a foursome is formed to investigate;
They discover a small place called Chuxiong
It was only about a half mile away.

We had one Chinese fellow in our group
Fluent in both Mandarin and the New Kunming;
These folks spoke something in between,
And this guy understood not one single thing!

Which mattered not, because they gave us chicken
And a big tub of fried (and cold) rice;
I fell in love with China that day,
(And learned what it meant to be nice.)

Our Pilot-Captain told them the plane was theirs,
(He didn't think Chennault would mind)
About three in the morning came another surprise,
Two jeeps came sailing thru, and Convoy five was close behind.

One can go to Harvard or Yale,
Study under the World's best minds;
You could get three degrees and a doctorate,
And not learn what some simple words mean,
----like "Kind."

Robert Maloney

Sister Sal

Her name was really Sally N., but at
Her first meeting, (I was there, too,)
Some guy hollers across the room,
"Hey, Sal, coffee's ready, how about you?"

Tall, slim, a bit nervous, Sally looks pretty good,
But her dark eyes tell another tale;
She said she couldn't complete the "nun run,"
And that's not easy to fail!

They went from convent to convent,
By whatever means I don't know,
But, half the time everyone's waiting,
For Sally McCarthy to show.

But Sally never gave up her faith,
Or the need to teach kids, you see;
So, her drinking aside, she went to school,
And earned a Master's degree.

By the time Sal got to twenty-eight
She was divorced with one little girl;
Being witty and pretty didn't help her,
Until the day she thought, "I'll give AA a whirl."

Now this happened back in the '70s,
When the booze took hold and held her;
And I didn't see her again until the '90s
She was teaching, and a Presbyterian Elder!

87

"Stand Me Up" Annie

Thal's was in the district called Hongkew,
It was down a long dark alley,
A place only a few locals knew,
And it stunk like an abandoned galley.

Two murders had taken place there
In less than a week, I'd heard;
Lots of people wouldn't dare,
We thought that was absurd.

You heard all sorts of bullshit,
Here in Shanghai's Hongkew;
Some made sense and seemed to fit,
Like this lady at Thal's that we knew.

Yes, I mean Stand-Me-Up-Annie
Who cooked and did the dishes;
Hung around, wiggled her fanny,
And ready to tend to your wishes.

One night my friend Al insisted
On trying to get her to bed;
She demurred but the kid persisted,
And guess where that finally led!

She took him to an old dumb waiter,
That took them to her den,
And it wasn't long (sooner than later)
Before they showed up, again.

Al said they did it twice,
Both times while standing up.
Twice because he was so nice, but
"She doesn't want to get knocked up."

Abe and Connie

They met in AA, and I remember the day
He told me they're getting hitched;
I said, "You're a lucky man, Abe,
I guess she got your best pitch!"

Abe laughed and said, "Well, you know her;
She's a member of the North Beach Group;
Her name is Connie and sponsors young gals
She calls, the 'Bikini Loop Group'."

"We're attached to the same Realty Office,
And frequently work on the same deals;
At our meetings, or when we show condos,
We relate; we know how each other feels."

The two fell madly in love,
(Their drinking had been pretty severe)
But, now they were blessed from above.
And they were both totally sincere.

She was a Smith College grad,
From Connecticut society, I think;
While Abe was builder of Strip Malls
One with a big skating rink.

And Abe was a Korean War Vet,
So we had more than booze to discuss;
I had been in China during World War Two;
Comparing notes was an absolute must.

High interest rates at the wrong time,
Got Abe out of his strip mall dream;
So he came down south and sold real estate,
And said so long to Ohio and Jim Beam.

Today, Abe's back up north
Building houses for Homes for Humanity,
Skies every winter (his favorite joy),
And defying the laws of gravity.

His beautiful Connie passed a few years back;
An AA Angel, now badly missed;
But, Abe carries on sponsoring,
Building, (and, ---well it's too long a list!)

How I think of them both every day!
And how they smiled and helped others;
(Throughout a batch of trials and tribulations),
Two of my favorite brothers.

The Attic Affair

We were up in a neighbor's attic;
Me, my friend and Pearl;
She said, "It's so romantic,
Two boys and only one girl."

"I want to kiss only one boy
To see if it's really fun,
So whoever has the biggest toy
Will be the lucky one."

Well, I was five and too confused;
But, Artie was six and ready;
Pearl was seven and highly amused
"Maybe I'm too young to go steady."

So, down came my knickers
And Artie's too,
Sally got a bad case of snickers,
Saying, "Here's what you have to do."

"You two take out your ding dings,
While I go find a ruler;"
Well, I was sweating bullets,
And Artie was not much cooler.

So, downstairs goes Pearl; then
While our things are hanging out,
Artie gives his a twirl!
Down below, we hear her mother shout!

"Why do you need the ruler, hon?"
I say, "Let's get out out of here."
Artie says, "But we ain't quite done?"
I'd never known such fear.

Then we hear the foot steps from below,
And we know that isn't Pearl;
Artie says, "Quick to the window,
That's sure no little girl!"

The house was two stories high,
Plus the attic we're standing in;
I say, "Art, you think we can fly?
No? Then I think we're in trouble again."

My Mom will get mad, I'm sure of that,
And she doesn't get mad very often;
But this time she'll use her baseball bat,
And I'll wind up in Granny's old coffin.

Well, Artie's then saying "Well, hello."
To Pearl's very mad mommy
Who's shielding our friend, who is down below,
And I'm getting sick to my tummy.

"Put on your pants, kids," she says,
"This party's come to an end,
And I'll see your mothers one of these days
On that you can depend."

Fast forward, to the end of the war;
It's February of forty-six.
I'm having a drink at the Tooth and Claw
Checking the new social mix.

I haven't seen this old town
Since the summer of thirty-nine;
But, now it's a place of world renown,
This great old home town of mine.

I'm visiting an old friend or two,
We've been seated in this crowded café.
The town is filled by another crew;
Students at study and at play.

Suddenly, I'm seized by a female stare,
She's sitting with two other girls;
It's the same mass of gorgeous blonde hair
Fixed in the same thirties curls.

Then she took her little thumb;
Held it high over the table.
I laughed until I was almost numb,
I was looking at Miss Betty Grable!

The Ring

Early summer, nineteen forty-eight,
We're making plans to be wed.
The place was Wetzlar, Germany,
I had met this old soldier named Fred.

Fred had been a Wehrmacht general
But, retired after world war one.
He was now well over eighty,
He was trying to sell his old gun.

I met him through my wife-to-be,
She'd been allowed to move there.
(Civilians were still not free, and
You couldn't just go anywhere.)

The General's wife was not that old,
Maybe around fifty-five,
And seemed to spend a lot of time
Trying to keep the old fellow alive.

Well, I had no use for the man's old gun,
(I wasn't mad at anyone)
But I really was anxious to find a ring,
And it couldn't be just any old thing.

One night Ruth, that was her name,
Knocked on Erika's door.
She said she'd sell her ring to us,
I almost fell through the floor.

I asked her what she wanted,
She said one dollar was all;
She wanted Erika to have it,
Then Erika started to bawl.

This was Germany in '48,
We'd been at each others throats,
But people are people everywhere,
And we all had a wonderful toast!

Mouse & His Folks

Mouse was born on a bedspread so worn
His little toes got caught in a stitch;
The Mid-Wife was pleased and gave him a squeeze,
While daddy crooned, "He's a cute little son of a bitch!"

Mommy was not amused---more likely a little abused;
How in the world could she do this again?
Instead of getting free, now comes number three,
And look at his Dad's stupid grin!

The father's name was Orville Pratt,
sometimes known as Pratt the Rat;
His creditors thought that was fitting;
His bills always late, way past due date.
Because job after job he kept quitting.

In fact, when Eileen first met Orville
She probably did smell a rat!
No, not literally of course,
But the guy was weird, with a handsome beard,
And behaving sometimes like a brat.

She was a CNA, went to work every day
At the Rehab Clinic where they'd met;
He was in because of booze and such,

But, she had him in a daze,
So he asked, "Are you married My Pet?"
Now, it was she walking around in a haze.

She was drawn to him like no other;
It only took about another week,
Until she was ready to be mistress and mother!
One nurse said, "Eileen is crazy about this freak."

Finally came that day, Pratt was out and in AA,
and their wedding was quite an affair;
Ex-drunks on one side, pretty nurses on the other
And gosh, I think even the Director was there.

So, Pratt's tab got paid, and he got laid.
And, wow, how easily she conceived!
It was "Hello, good day?" and another little tyke got made,
And they loved each bundle received!

When Mouse was three he could paint a tree,
Some friends said, "He's a young Dali"
By the time he was ten, Orville asked a close friend
To help open a "Little Kid's Gallery."

They invited the whole town, served cookies and buns,
While the old folks oohed and awhed;
The youngest was ten, the oldest thirteen,
Second best was this kid called Bernard.

Bernie drew cartoons of cats blowing balloons,
And cows giving milk into a Wheaties dish;
But as good as he was, he was second because,
Mouse's work was called Cavendish.

The place took off, with nary a scoff
From the snobs on Blueberry Hill;
But with the good art, came a caveat;
Orville was hanging at Tony's West End Grill.

Eileen was worried, deep inside her was buried
Scenes more than ten years old,
She had always thought of the day in fifty-eight
When Orville had "Come in from out of the Cold."

Then came the night, after a bedroom fight,
When she asked him "what's going on?
You're at the West End more than you're home,
And don't insult me with your bullshit con!"

"I haven't been to a meeting in weeks,
My sponsor's headed for Viet Nam,
One night we had a party for him
I had a few pops after he'd gone."

Aileen was glad he'd not gotten mad,
And for awhile the guy's off the hook;
He got a new sponsor named Frank, and
A copy of the latest Big Book.

Frank had "been to the post" more often than most
And it was like looking in a tall glass;
So easy to remember, when he was a new member
Being broke and flat on his ass.

I don't want to say, Frank saved the day,
But the facts became known to all;
"I told him, 'Fake it, 'until you make it'
And if the thinking's off center, just give me a call."

When Mouse reached sixteen, he was being seen
As a world known artist-to-be;
While Orville and Aileen were also being seen
As lovers and again, alcohol-free.

The Big "O"

The guy walks in, says, "I'm Rockford O'Reilly;"
He immediately became the "Big O".
He goes on, "and please don't call me Rocky;
That gets kind of old, don't you know!"

I said, "We'll call you what ever you want,
What do they call you in New York."
His accent was vintage Brooklyn, and
He said, "Mostly, it's just plain, Rock."

We all said, "sounds good" and went from there;
He was an agent for some football players,
Had a yacht as big as a house, and was
A part time Preacher; (said he'd lead us in prayers.)

I said, "Rock, this is AA; how long
Have you been in the program"?
He said, "I'm not really an alcoholic,
Just an evangelic, everyday, layman."

"I come down for the winter, and my boat's
Up at the end of Captiva Shores;
I like this church, and want to spread
The word within and beyond these doors."

Kelley's looking at his cigarette,
Puts it out and lights another;
Then cracks, "Mister, case you didn't know
Most of us already got a Mother."

Well, the Rock was in shock
And said, "Well that's only you."
I said, "Well, we appreciate your good will,
But, this is a closed meeting, for you."

"Friday, there's an open meeting, right here;
If you want to come and listen,"
I went on, "But this meeting is closed,
And you should know, AA is not a mission."

"But look, you can buy the book,
Called Alcoholics Anonymous;
It's less than six bucks and I think there's one
Over there by old Charley Adonis."

It was nearly a year later, when one hot
Night, I decide to go on over to YANA;
Friday was an open speaker group,
Filled wall to wall, and usually hot as a sauna.

Sitting near the front, I see this man,
And I think I recognize the guy;
I put on my best smile, and get up
To go, and ask this big fellow "why?"

Well, he sees me, too, and winds his way thru
The crowd and gets to me near the back;
"I can see you're no sap, and saw thru that crap
And my name is not Rockford, it's Jack!"

"Booze had me crazy, and things being hazy,
I didn't think I was just another drunk;
Yes, I was once a preacher, but never very good,
And most said my sermons were junk."

"But I do have a boat, but barely afloat,
How I got it here I don't know;
It was part of a dream, or maybe a scheme,
To turn things around and even grow."

I lost track of Big Jack, but behind his back,
I had asked a couple of sailors I knew,
To, maybe say hello, maybe get to know,
This guy who came right out of the blue.

The last I heard, (from a little bird)
Was that Jack was on Fort Myers Beach;
He had registered a "sack" with a running back
And a five foot Lin Lee had him on a leash.

Calvin and Sophia

They came, they stayed, later they played
In the sand on this barrier reef;
They had been wed, and it had been said,
Hired by a Bishop named O'Keeffe.

Calvin was a man who had a plan,
And Sophia went along all the way;
To care for the mansion, with hard work and passion
And learn of the sea day by day.

This was nineteen forty-eight, Selma a long time away,
And black folks were not always welcome
To houses like this, (a fact they couldn't miss),
No matter how pretty or handsome.

In time the pair, who were always there,
Built their own little six room house;
Bishop O'Keeffe gave them a hand, deeded them land---
Heck, even stocked some of the land with grouse!

Soon the grouse all croaked (well, some may have been choked)
But the deed was duly noted
Which didn't change the need to arrange
The disposal of the smelly and bloated.

It wasn't long before two girls were born,
One right after the other;
Cal said, "First there was one, then more fun!"
("Though, I was half rooting for a brother.")

Over the years, lots of laughs and tears
Filled the house on this little island;
The girls sometimes prayed ('tho more often they played)
On the beach they called their play land.

A ferry got started, and each day they carted
Themselves, and their gear to the dock;
When they got off the ferry, they were met by "Aunt Mary"
Born, she once said, of Old West Tennessee stock.

Alas came the day, when things weren't the same;
Cal's trips to shore became over night,
"The seas are too rough, the boat's not big enough,
And those sharks are a real scary sight."

Sophia called a friend, who was now on the mend
From a brawl at a mainland saloon,
Where she tended bar for her Ma and Pa, and she said,
"Yes, Soph, Cal's here on week day afternoons."

Now Sophia didn't fool around, she went to work and found,
A guy in town who was AA;
He said, "Get him over, it won't be all clover,
But we'll see what Cal's got to say."

Calvin was shocked---he was on the clock!
When Sophia told him what was what;
"I don't care if it's fair, you just get there,
And some day you'll praise God you got caught."

She then emphasized, to his surprise, that
Ramona and Jenn were in on the plot,
And the twelve year old twins, said it again,
"Dad, you and Mom's all we got!"

To the surprise of all, Cal made the call
To this fellow called Fred at AA.
Fred said, "I've got a little boat, and if she's afloat,
I'll be at your dock about eight."

Cal got home about eleven, looking like 'seventh heaven',
And vowing he'd do what Fred said,
Which was "fake it until you make it"
And, "I've got a nice extra bed."

"I hope you can stay, with me a few days
So I can introduce you around;
Say Saturday and Sunday, I'll take off
Monday, and we'll check out the meetings downtown."

You ask him today, Calvin would say,
"I felt at home right from day one,
Not one bit of flack, what with my being black,
It's crazy, but it was kind of fun."

In that first full week, Cal got a peek
At what AA was all about;
He wanted a drink, but then would think,
That would feel like striking out.

After Calvin came home, he swore he'd never roam
And leave his wife and girls again;
He was also met by a man soaking wet
Who had been scuba diving with Ramona and Jenn.

Bishop O'Keeffe said, "I talked to Fred,
And he wants to start a new meeting
Here on the island, maybe on our land, but
I told him we'd been taking a beating!"

"There's no way of telling, but we're thinking of selling
The upkeep's not cheap; ---well, you know;
Like we don't pay you guys enough,
And we were sure this island would grow!"

So they worked it out, an unknown amount,
Was gathered from who knows where;
To buy the place and put on a new face
It's now known as AlkyCare!

I hear Cal's still alive, able to survive,
Thanks to his girls and AA;
He may not live long, but we'd be wrong
To think he's not having a "Good Day!"

Cadillac Kate

From behind the bed/chair, I could see the red hair
And she didn't really look that great;
Then she opened her eyes, and to my surprise,
I was looking at Cadillac Kate!

It was back in eighty-two that Katie joined the crew
At the Sanibel Friday Night Meeting
I recall her sailing in, wearing a sly grin,
And then kissing us all in her greeting

She said, "I just got here, 'tho my car threw a gear
And is back in a Georgia shop."
We were all enthralled, and as I recall,
She'd left it with a Valdosta cop.

Well, she flew to Valdosta (God knows what it cost her)
And picked up her car, and her cop;
So that's how Kate got her new name and mate,
But, now it was about her last stop.

As I reminisced, she asked to be kissed
So I came close to her cheek, and said "Kate"
I touched her bare shoulder, felt it get colder
But my kiss, alas, was too late.

At which point I looked up, and there holding a cup,
Of what looked like a warm cup of tea,
A nurse shedding a tear, saying, "excuse me, dear;
But that lady's was named Anna Lee."

Robbie

Robbie was a farmer, also a charmer,
From a place in Iowa called Ames;
He had the dough, including cash flow,
And was ready for some South Beach games.

He met a little chick, she looked dumb as a stick,
And she fell for his charm right away;
Both were newly sober, and looked each other over,
Before getting it on one fine day.

They really clicked, and decided to stick
Together, at least for awhile;
He for some action, but with out any traction,
And she with her killer smile.

It took a week before this geek,
Is thinking of maybe a trio;
Then with the next breath he's thinking meth
And his new friend is thinking, "Weirdo."

Now Kathy Randle (that's her handle)
Is thinking she made a mistake,
Getting it on with this ding dong
Who was nutty as last year's fruitcake.

After a short while, with the sex getting more wild,
Kathy said "What am I doing?"
Her answer was short, she was being bought
And was scared of the guy she'd been screwing.

She called AA, and right away
Two guys and a girl showed up;
She said she didn't think, that she'd had a drink
But was not sure why she threw up.

They took a walk, had a nice talk,
And the girl Dottie, took her home;
While the two men, Artie and Ben,
Went to see Robbie alone.

Not much was said, Robbie's in bed
With some floosee named Flo;
Both were wasted, and the whole scene tasted
Like rotten eggs eaten slow.

Artie and Ben decided then,
This was "maybe not a good time;"
So, under a glass tumbler, they left a number,
And on top was one thin dime.

Now, Kathy stayed with Dot a few days,
Then drove back to her Mom in Naples;
As I sit here, she's been sober a full year,
And selling computer stuff at Staples.

It took some time, before Rob used the dime,
He'd found under the glass of booze;
He was back in Ames, (things weren't the same)
But in general it was pretty good news.

He had ninety days, and other ways
Like being honest for a change,
And making the call, (to Miami and all)
From his home back there on the range!

Ben said, "Tonight's your first chip, so here's a tip:
Keep it in your pocket at all times."
Then Ben hung up, and with his coffee cup,
Thanked God he'd been carrying that dime!

The Day Loren Quit

This has been my home group,
For almost twenty years;
My second since I moved here
(Sometimes you have to shift gears.)

The last one, I lived on an Island
(No point in saying which one);
This was Loren's first Home Group, I think;
Sort of a guy who was not much fun.

Like a bunch of people in this area,
Loren was sort of a recluse;
He was quite a handsome lad
And looked a lot like the actor, Tom Cruise.

Each week he would bring a folder
It carried his new book and fortune;
It never ever left his sight
It was, he said, that important.

But nobody had the time, you see,
To read Loren's manuscript;
They were busy staying sober,
And wouldn't know a quote from encrypt.

Loren had a job, somewhere at a Mall
Connected to security and such;
He told someone it was menial,
And, he said it didn't pay very much.

His comments were usually negative
He always seemed above it,
Sometimes referring to the program,
As "living a life of horse shit."

I asked him one day, "Got a sponsor?"
His answer was, quickly, "What for?
If I decide to drink I won't want
Someone hanging around my front door."

Then one March night he came early;
"Someone stole part of my book;
It's not in my car, or at the Mall
And I don't know where else to look."

"How about home," someone offered,
"Isn't that where you write your book?"
"I'm living with a good friend, and
I know he's not a crook."

Later that evening, the meeting's half over,
The guy next to Loren says, "Thank You,"
And it's now Loren's turn to say,
"My name is Loren, and this is to say, "I'm through."

Loren then made a "resignation" speech;
And this may have been the first
Since Bill W and Bob got together
If not, it sure was one of the worst.

He said, "Some bastard stole my book;
One of the most important parts;
This part was the ending, and I know
It had to be one of you old farts."

After he picked up his hat,
(A Yankees cap as I recall),
He strode out like King Arthur,
Straight out of the Baptist front hall.

A few minutes later, the meeting ended,
We headed for the coffee and cake;
Then I heard Corky's voice saying,
"Oh, Bob, look at this, fercrissake."

It was Loren's portfolio and folder
Lying behind the big urn;
We never knew who stashed it, and
I'm glad we never did learn.

Almost a year later, my pal Corky
Finally solved the mystery;
He'd been part of the clean-up crew
And decided this might be history.

Most papers, were blank, he said,
But some had what looked like calculus
As well as sketches of a ladies head;
There was also, a note on the very
last page, that said:
"The real Loren Hardy is dead."

Corky revealed, he'd gone to the police
The day after finding the papers;
He'd been advised to keep silent
Although it was maybe just foolish capers.

Nobody ever saw Loren again
Either at the Mall or anywhere,
And surely not at any other meetings;
But I still wonder: "Why did he leave them there?"

Afterword

Some of these poems and ballads reflect Alcoholics Anonymous as it was during the 1960's and into the 1990's. There are suggestions that the membership of this world wide organization has stagnated; that it contains, today, about 2,000,000 members, similar numbers to what they were ten years ago.

My own observations confirm this: A closed meeting I now attend, albeit rarely, has about ten active members, and a normal meeting attendance of six or seven. In the 1990's, when I was a regular member, there was never a night when there were not at least 50 people in the house; sometimes more.

As I wrote these ballads, with names, places and circumstances altered, I realized more and more that a lot has changed since those days---especially going back to the 1960's. Considering the changes in the various health care laws and the emergence of re-hab centers, I don't think that's surprising. And welcome! My own experiences speak to these changes in many ways, In 1958, my employer's health care experts had me confined to a hospital south of Boston, where I received shock treatments every other day. I went AWOL from this place after a couple of weeks, and was then summarily dismissed from their wonderful program! And a week prior to my coming in to AA in August of 1960, I was treated at the New Hampshire State Hospital in Concord, N.H. They kept me three days, and decided (I guess) that I was probably not going into DT's, so they called my wife to come and get me. After staying sober, in AA, for two months, I was hired by General Motors.

I hope you enjoy the poems/ballads. If you think you may have a problem, you probably do. In which case, please call AA. Max and

Grady and Al aren't around anymore, but there are 2,000,000 others who are ready, willing and able to help. Use the rest of this page for those early names and phone numbers. Thirty or forty years down the road, you may want to look them over.

About the Author

Robert E. Maloney was the first person in his family to be born in a hospital (Keene, NH---1924). He served in the US Army from March 1943 until December 1948. Uncle Sam happily provided passage, with beer and cigarette money, to some exotic places like, Bombay and Ledo (India), Bhamo and Lashio (Burma), and Kunming and Shanghai (China). Thanks to the GI Bill, he received two degrees (Industrial Engineering and Engineering Management) from Northeastern University.

He married two wonderful women, both now deceased. He made a decent living, enjoyed spending most of it, as a mechanical engineer (during the cold war) and as a conniving stockbroker during the roaring eighties. His children are up north swatting bugs and cursing the New England and New York traffic.

His third book is due out on the heels of this one. It is his memoir titled, **WWII - My World War Two story in 3 parts**. He expects it to outsell **FROM HERE TO ETERNITY**, and says, "If it doesn't, at this stage of my game (age 91), who will give a damn one way or the other.

His first book published earlier in 2015 is also a story peotry book from his days in the military as a young soldier. Visit Amazon.com for a print copy or an ebook of **LOST IN BURMA**.

Connect with Robert

Robert's Publisher
http://SpiderBooksPublishing.com

Robert's Facebook
https://www.facebook.com/bob.maloney.315

Robert's Website
http://ftmyersbob.blogspot.com

Other books by R.E. Maloney

Lost in Burma
http://amzn.to/1HEE2on

www.ingramcontent.com/pod-product-compliance
Lightning Source LLC
Chambersburg PA
CBHW060940040426
42445CB00011B/947